Poems from the Future Artopia:

A Manifesto in Ekphrasis

By J. Martin Strangeweather

Cover artwork by J. Martin Strangeweather
Graphic design by Dustin Myers
Published by the Santa Ana Literary Association
Printed in the United States of America
ISBN 978-0-578-39848-8
Library of Congress Control Number: 2022905533

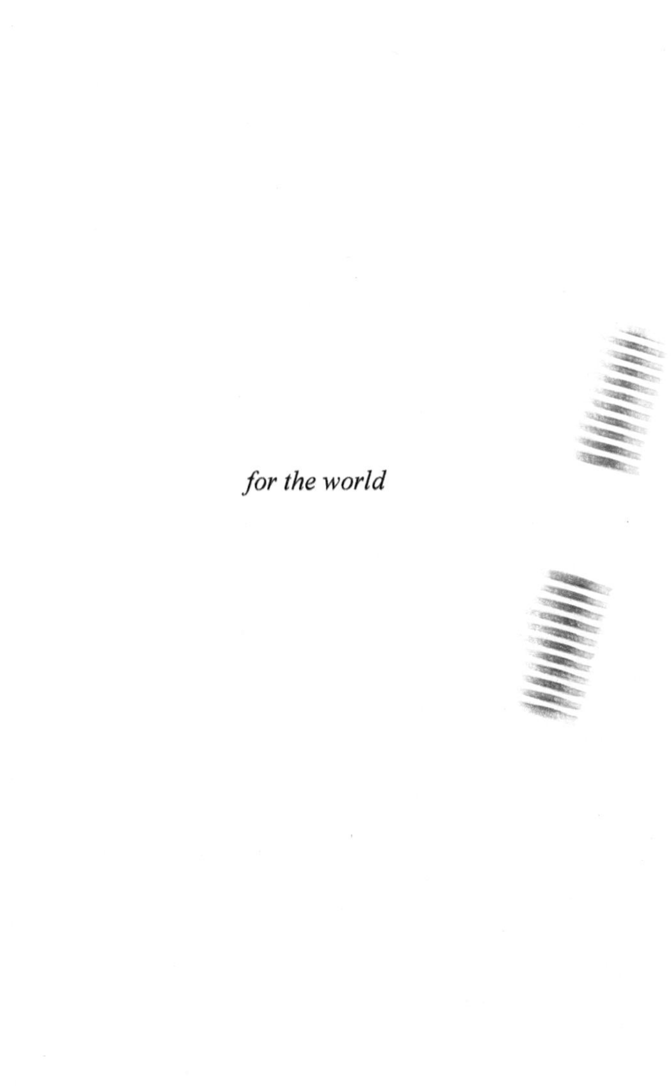

for the world

The Emperor Wears No-Clothes™

Olga Kalashnikov's see-through tuxedos
sell for ten million dollars U.S.,
and that's not including the bowtie.

Every high-profile world leader owns one,
partly to support Olga's cause,
mainly to support their insatiable need
for public adoration
and social stratification.

Each suit takes Olga a year to produce,
working ten hours a day,
including weekends and holidays.
Custom-made, completely handsewn
from 100% recycled plastic,
which she converts into a clear microfiber fabric
that's durable yet breathable.
No one knows how she does it,
and she's not telling.

Ten million dollars a suit,
distributed freely to the country's poorest babushkas,
keeping almost nothing for herself,
just enough to live in modest comfort.
She's made thirty-two tuxedos to date.
That's $320,000,000 given away in $100,000 donations
to Russia's destitute elderly population.

Olga turned 70 this year.
She doesn't think she has many tuxedos left in her,
but her list of backorders goes on
for more than a hundred years.
She says she'll take on an apprentice
when she feels ready to retire
to the earth,
but only someone she can trust
never to sell the secret of the wondrous fabric
to Gucci or Versace
or Levi Strauss.

The tuxedos themselves are surreal masterpieces,
double-breasted coats with peaked lapels

and vented sides,
faceted buttons of Swarovski crystal,
spread-collared pleated shirts
with plackets and French cuffs
woven from the same invisible fabric
as the jacket and trousers,
gossamer threads catching iridescent rainbows
from every angle.
Nothing but a satiny sheen between the eye and its fancy.

Olga the humble seamstress from Volgograd,
her patient process, her fantastical product,
the redistribution of wealth to those who need it most,
it's more than creative genius,
it's creative love,
from start to finish.

She calls her line of tuxedos No-Clothes™.
The kings and presidents of many countries
wear No-Clothes™,
and the irony isn't lost on anyone.

Imagine a roomful of dignitaries
with their naked truth on avant-garde display,
proving they have nothing to hide
or be ashamed of.

This is the revolutionary art of the 22nd century,
if not the 21st.

The Ark Series

There's a battleship in the Sonoran Desert.
Retired Vice Admiral Roy Stewart is waging a war
against homelessness.

After removing the anti-aircraft guns
and missile launchers,
the USS *Iowa* (BB-61) was cut in half,
and both halves of the battleship were placed upright
with their decks facing each other.
A relic of war converted into mass housing.
Mass housing converted into art.

The hull halves are spaced a hundred feet apart
from each other,
with four rickety swings and a rusted seesaw in-between.

The stern half of the ship-cum-housing
is called Stern Side.
The bow half of the ship-cum-housing
is called Bow Side.

The Vice Admiral himself resides in a cabin
on the 4th floor of Bow Side.
The locals call him Captain Roy.
Captain Roy lives with his first mate,
Gobby Robbie.

Captain Roy is waging a war
against neglect,
having seen too many loyal sea dogs abandoned
to the streets
once their service,
their usefulness,
their duty,
their strength,
was done.

No wife, no children,
no surviving family members to speak of,
upon his retirement
Roy Stewart had only one thing left
anchoring him to this world:
he had a mission.

Having served his country honorably for 35 years
(never once asking, never once telling),
Roy Stewart had made many powerful connections,
some of whom were in charge
of decommissioned naval vessels.

The gigantic artwork is simply titled *Ark #1*,
but the locals who squat there have taken to calling it
New Eden.

New Eden's upturned hull halves are completely covered
in black solar panels,
with fifty wind turbines mounted along the perimeter
of each half of the bisected deck,
providing free energy year-round.
And there's free wifi!
It's a squatter's paradise.
Daily tours help cover the cost of upkeep
and the monthly water bill:
$20 for adults,
$10 for students,

$5 for children 15 years and under.
Open 10 a.m. to 5 p.m. Monday through Friday,
closed on weekends and major holidays.

Each half of the battleship is a forty-story structure, each capped with its own water tower. Each forty-story structure contains 1,250 identical housing units, or cabins. Each cabin comes with an air conditioner, a mini refrigerator, a military-issue folding cot, a sink with hot and cold running water, and a stove. Each cabin door has a key code lock. Each half of the battleship contains a gym on the 10th floor and a large indoor public swimming pool (82'x164') at the top level. Each floor contains two shared bathrooms: four toilets and two urinals for the men's room, six toilets for the women's room, and two shared shower facilities: one for those identifying as men, the other for those identifying as women, five stalls in each.

There's a library full of donated books
on the 3rd floor of Bow Side.
There's also a church on the 3rd floor of Bow Side,
and it's packed every Sunday.

There are even free laundry facilities
on the 2nd floor of both halves of New Eden,
but good luck finding a washer or dryer that's not in use.

Most of the hallways and stairwells are covered in graffiti
and tend to smell of urine.
Some floors reek of marijuana
and other more exotic substances.
Both halves of New Eden have an elevator,
though one or the other is always closed for repairs.

New Eden employs ten janitors,
one plumber,
one electrician,
one elevator mechanic,
and two security guards
(nicknamed Sheriff Nottingham and Deputy Doolittle
by the locals),
all of whom live onsite.

Some locals call themselves Edenites,
others refer to themselves as Roy's Rejects,

but everyone aboard knows they're shipmates.

We make up the objects,
And the objects make up us.

Many of the locals have come to adopt the look
and mannerisms of scallywag pirates.
Variations of the Jolly Roger
are spraypainted on every level.
Steer clear of the Flying Dutchmen,
a gang of tweakers who've monopolized the 33rd floor
on the Stern Side of New Eden.

New Eden's citizenry consists mostly of alcoholics
and drug addicts,
most of whom are veterans,
along with a smattering of artists,
anarchists,
poets,
prostitutes
(there's a red-light district on the 31st floor of Stern Side),
and practitioners of black magick.

Neo-Nazis and assholes in general aren't welcome
in New Eden,
but they still end up here
from time to time.

The rules are few:
Don't physically hurt your neighbors or you'll get booted.
Don't steal from your neighbors or you'll get booted.
Don't get caught.

All cabins are on a first come, first served basis.
If you are gone for more than thirty days,
your key code will be changed
and any possessions found in your lodging
will be added to the free zone.

The cabins on the fortieth floor are reserved
for "incomers" (people with incomes + newcomers).
Affording the best views of the surrounding desolation,
New Eden's topmost cabins are rented out
to curiosity seekers for $25 per night,
the funds of which go to pay the onsite employees.

There are thirty rentable cabins on Stern Side,
And twenty-five on Bow Side.
Vacancies are rare.
Book your stay at least a month in advance.

Other works in the Ark Series include an oil tanker
located a hundred miles outside of Portland, Oregon,
titled *Ark #2*, christened Big Rock Candy Mountain
by the local squatters,
and an aircraft carrier in the middle of the Bronx,
titled *Ark #3*, or Skyville by its inhabitants.

Chavy's Place

The most celebrated and beloved artist
of the 22nd century
is a quiet seventeen-year-old girl from Cambodia
who prefers going barefoot.
Her name is Chavy Nei Prei,
and she detests shoes.
"If you have to wear shoes there,
I don't want to go," she says.

Chavy makes sturdy shelters and palatial estates
in the middle of nowhere
for free
using natural materials
scavenged from the jungle.
No magic, miracles, or superpowers needed,
just a lot of dedication and a little know-how.

Location is key.
She only constructs shelters in remote places
near a source of water,

never further than half a kilometer away.
Chavy stays one week in every house she builds,
to test its livability,
then moves on.

Chavy prefers her own company
to the company of others,
saying people in general are "very draining."

Men in uniforms burned down her village
when she was very young.
Men in uniforms executed her father and brother
in front of her.
Men in uniforms did something unspeakable
to her mother.
Men in uniforms did something unspeakable
to her sister.
Men in uniforms did something unspeakable
to her, so unspeakable she wanted to die.
But she couldn't.
Her family needed her.
Her community needed her.

Boundless compassion arose
from the ashes of her village.

Chavy has developed her own unique
architectural style,
which can only be described as
primitive surreal futurism,
like if Hieronymus Bosch
collaborated with George Lucas
to recreate Hobbiton.

When asked about her creative process,
Chavy says, "The materials call out to me,
and nature shows me what to design."
Her houses look like bizarre otherworldly creatures.
"Everything I make is alive," she says.

First World Dream is one of her most famous pieces,
taking four months to complete.
First World Dream is a four-story apartment complex
resembling a cross between a squid and a snail,

built next to a waterfall.
There are four spacious living quarters on each level,
for a total of sixteen dwellings,
each shaped bulbous like a bloated stomach,
each with their own balcony,
each furnished with a wicker rocking chair
and a bamboo table
handmade by Chavy.
And that's not all.
Each apartment has a bathroom
with a western-style toilet (a sit-down toilet)
made from bamboo,
the rim of which is made from grass and clay subsoil
mixed into plaster.
Chavy has ingeniously diverted
a small section of the waterfall
to rig the apartment complex
with bamboo plumbing.

The isolated village of Saambok Baksaei
is Chavy's most ambitious project to date,
taking nearly half a year to complete.

She built the village singlehandedly,
when she was only fourteen-years-old.
That was three years ago.
The village is still standing today, fully inhabited,
in an area known to flood every monsoon season.
From a distance
the village looks like twelve giant bacteriophages
gathered in a circle,
their bodies covered in spikes
like the spiny skin of a pufferfish.
Each of the icosahedral huts is raised
on six ten-foot-high poles
placed at acute angles.
Saambok Baksaei means “The Bird Nests” in Khmer.

Shangri-La is Chavy’s most recent masterpiece,
taking her three month to complete.
It’s a three-story, ten-bedroom mansion
made from bamboo,
with an Olympic-size swimming pool on the rooftop.
The pool has a waterslide on one end,
and a bamboo diving board on the other.

Shangri-La is completely covered in earthen tiles
growing wild with grass and wildflowers.
The overall exterior looks like a combination
of cockroach and turtle,
with ten eyelike windows
bearing intricate latticework screens
hand-carved by Chavy.

Simpler dwellings
(lozenge-shaped wicker huts and
onion-domed mud houses)
only take her about a week to construct.
The only tool she uses is her timeworn hand axe,
the only tool she trusts,
its rusty blade used for cutting and digging,
its stout handle used for hammering.
This was her father's axe.
She also carries a clay pot everywhere she goes,
which she made herself.
A hand axe and a clay pot. These are her only possessions.
She does not use nails in her constructions.
Vines and bark fiber for twine suffice.

Her process isn't a secret.

Step One: clear the ground,
removing weeds and dead branches
and other obstacles
that keep new ideas from taking shape.

Step Two: establish stability,
digging holes in which to place sturdy posts.
Chavy scoops the earth away with her bare hands,
setting aside any large rocks
which can be used to make an oven.
She doesn't take the dirt for granted.
Later it will be mixed
with leaves and grass and water
to become a sort of cement.
She gathers fallen logs
and hacks off their branches.
She whittles one end of each log to a point
and hammers them into position.

Step Three: construct a framework
from whatever materials are locally available:
bamboo, thick branches, stripped logs, and so on.
Tie slats horizontally across the posts.
"It's like building a birdcage," she says.

Chavy makes her own ladders
from bamboo.

Step Four: reinforce the framework,
smearing mud-grass mortar over the slats
and rubbing the surfaces to a smooth finish,
or fashion wall panels woven in wicker fashion
from strips of bark soaked in water
to make them pliable.

Chavy weaves her own baskets and nets
from reeds.

Step Five: create a weather-resistant
and inviting
facade.

For example:
Weave palm fronds into thatching
and brace the thatching with bamboo slats.

Chavy builds her own ovens
from soil and stones.

Step Six: add a pool,
because who doesn't like a pool?
To create a pool,
Chavy draws a rectangle on the ground,
digs out the rectangle to a depth of one meter,
lines the rectangular pit with posts,
ties bamboo slats across the posts,
leaving the top of the posts sticking up
about five centimeters (i.e., four fingers)
above the ground to create a lip,
then she plasters the pit
with mud-grass cement
using her bare hands as trowels.
After the cement dries,
she takes sap from the acacia tree

and uses it as a sealant.
After the sealant dries,
she takes pigment made from the chlorophyll of leaves
pulped in her clay pot with the handle of her axe,
and paints the pool a pleasant shade of green,
using her bare hands as brushes.

How does she fill the pool with water?
One potful at a time.

Chavy doesn't accept payment for her creations,
requesting all donations be sent to Wildlife Alliance,
a non-governmental organization
devoted to preserving the Cambodian rainforest.

Everyone is welcome to watch and learn from Chavy
as she builds her magnificent houses,
though she politely asks you
to refrain from taking pictures or video footage of her
while she's working.

She's been invited to give demonstrations
in Germany, France, and the United States,
but she refuses to leave Cambodia.
"Those people don't really need my help," she says.
"They just want to be entertained."

The King of Cambodia himself
endorses her interactive outdoor installation pieces,
mainly because her artworks have increased tourism
by 18%.

According to Chavy,
her greatest architectural achievement
remains a secret,
buried somewhere deep in the jungle
like a lost Angkor Wat.
She titled it *Chavy's Heart*.
No one has ever seen it,
but everyone trusts she's telling the truth
about its existence.
"It's too beautiful," she says of the work.
"It shouldn't exist in this world."

She took a vow never to reveal its location.
"You know how men are," she says.
"They're territorial, and selfish…
some men would kill to claim it as their own."
Chavy understands that someone will find it someday,
but she hopes by then it will be too dilapidated to covet.

The New Lou

Chinese fighter jets bombed the Louvre
during the Fourth World War.
Rather than rebuild the world's largest, most iconic
art museum,
the French government saw fit to leave it
the way it was—
brutally exposed,
and truthful.

The bombing fused the literal
with the figurative,
transforming all the masterpieces
into a single work of art,
an installation on the grandest of scales,
eleven thousand years in the making.

The demolished museum-cum-installation art
is called The New Lou.
The artist is simply credited as China.

The whole blasted site
is covered in a glass and steel dome
to protect what remains of the artworks
from further damage owing to the elements.

Walkways have been cleared through the wreckage,
but many areas are off-limits due to
unstable floors and ceilings.

You still have to pay a €20 entry fee.
Only €20 to feel something real.

The walls left standing
are blackened with blast marks,
but guards will still give you a warning
if you get too close to the art.

In what's left of the Richelieu Wing,
we find pieces of the Code of Hammurabi,
but not enough to answer this question:
if the Code of Hammurabi's wisdom is lost forever,
then what?

Making our way through the ruins
of the Denon Wing,
we come across the *Winged Victory of Samothrace*,
its wings blown off,
looking anything but victorious,
and the charred remnant of *Mona Lisa*,
her smile just a memory,
Liberty Leading the People in tatters.

Among the marble debris of the Sully Wing,
we greet the *Venus de Milo*,
now headless as well as armless,
and the Great Sphinx of Tanis,
not looking so great
with half its face gone.
Zeus lies in scorched rubble,
all the old gods and goddesses toppled.

A hundred centuries of well-crafted illusions
laid bare,
unearthing deeper layers of the artistic process

than the original artists
had intended:
the folly of man,
the peace of death,
the beauty of decay,
the silence of eternity.

Repurposed Love

It's simply called *The Toy Ball.*
A ball made from castoff baby dolls and teddy bears,
currently measuring over eight hundred feet in diameter,
painted uniformly white.

...like ghosts
  ...like faded memories
    ...haunting, and inescapable.

It took form in Manhattan, in the middle of Times Square.
No one knows who started it,
but it's been funded by the New York City Council
for the past ten years,
ever since the pandemic of 2112.

Over a million children died that year,
and that's just in the U.S.

Nowadays,
rather than throw away a doll
or stuffed animal that's been outgrown
or become ratty,
people from all over the country
donate their toys to The Ball Fund,
giving the toys a new life…
an afterlife.

The Toy Ball grows larger every year.
Every Winter Solstice, the toys that
have been donated throughout the year
are affixed to the artwork
and the whole thing gets a new coat of
weatherproof white paint.

People come year-round
to marvel at the ghostly colossus,
many of them trying to find their forfeited childhood
buried within the multitude of repurposed love.

Childhood memories piled high as a skyscraper,
toys dominate the Manhattan skyline
and blot out the sun.

Vote Vishnu

A man appeared in the slums of Mumbai,
planting fruit trees,
the fastest growing varieties:
fig,
papaya,
banana.
The man said his name had been stolen from him.

A man with no name
appeared in the backstreets of Mumbai,
watering various community gardens
sowed by his own hands
with the fastest growing vegetables:
radishes,
carrots,
tomatoes.
The man had no identification card,
saying only that he came from the north.

The man with no name was well-educated,
his rhetoric gave it away.
He spoke of different ways and better days that were
just around the corner.
But unlike others of his caste,
he worked as he spoke,
worked hard,
with his hands
and his heart.

A man with no name
appeared before the impoverished masses,
claiming he was an artist,
but he seemed more like a politician.
He said he was the founder of an art movement,
but the movement seemed more like a political party.

He asked the impoverished masses to vote for him
in the Maharashtra Legislative Assembly election,
and the impoverished masses asked
who's name should they write on the ballot?
He simply answered, "Vishnu."

A man named Vishnu
appeared before his fellow members
of the Mumbai South Lok Sabha constituency.
He presented his artistic vision
to the House of Parliament,
and the parliamentarians voted on it.

They voted in favor of art.

The large-scale installation piece
is titled *Project Regrowth.*
The idea is simple, the execution monumental:
Allow all the vegetation in Mumbai to grow
unimpeded for one year.
No pulling weeds.
No mowing grass.
No pruning bushes.
No cutting branches off trees,
unless they pose a threat.

Let the weeds sprout freely
from the asphalt cracks
and concrete crevices.
If sidewalks and roads become overgrown,
so be it.

Not only is the Indian government
funding the citywide project,
various nonprofit art organizations
from around the world
are contributing funds as well.
A majority of the funds go to employing
the poorest of Mumbai's citizenry
as city gardeners,
creating 100,000 new jobs.

The city gardeners plant saplings
and train vines to crawl
up traffic signals and electric poles,
storefronts and skyscrapers,
coloring the cityscape
blue with butterfly peas,

purple with morning glories,
pink with petunias,
and scarlet with bougainvillea.
Butterflies abound,
as do sunbirds and parakeets.

The city gardeners like to say
they are the hands of Vishnu.

When the yearlong art project was over,
the city was so lush
and paradisiacal that
everyone agreed
to stretch it out for another year,
and then another.

Mumbai was recently named one of
the most beautiful cities in the world
by Lonely Planet.
Tourism is up 400% from where it was
three years ago.

Untitled

It’s a nationwide performance art piece.
It’s a Scottish holiday.
It doesn’t really have a name.
You can call it whatever you want.
You can use it however you want.

Laws still apply during this holiday,
for the most part.

Some people call it National “Piss Off” Day,
others call it “Who Gives a Shit?” Day.
A lot of people know it as
Intergalactic Shroom Day.

On March Fourth
(a date chosen purely for its play on words),
for 24 hours,
everyone pretends to be real,
stopping the usage of all screen-based technology
(computers, smartphones, televisions)

and partaking in festivities such as
The Naming and The Telling.

It began in Glasgow,
initiated by The Untitled Collective,
a group of artists, actors, poets, and musicians.
The Untitled Collective organized a series
of “anti-scenes” and “be-outs”
at the turn of the 22nd century.

Performance art pieces are to the untitled holiday
as fireworks are to the Fourth of July,
which is ironic
for a day devoted to keeping things real.

The Naming:
Allow yourself to be
boldly
painfully
honest.
What’s the worst thing about you,
the thing you hide from people,

the thing you don't want people to
associate with your name?
Liar?
Cheater?
Hypocrite?
Pervert?
Poser?
This is what society makes of you.
It's okay. We're all basically the same.
Be who you're afraid of being.
Be who you really are,
at least for 24 hours.
Write your truer name across your forehead
in permanent marker,
knowing that nothing is truly permanent.

The Telling:
Allow yourself to be
boldly
painfully
honest
with your friends and family.

It’s a game of endurance.
How truthful can you get
before the point of no return?

No one works during this holiday
unless they feel like it,
and public nudity is strongly encouraged.

It’s an exercise in self-control.
It’s an exercise in letting go of all self-control.
If this sounds contradictory,
that’s because it’s real.

The untitled holiday even has
its own legendary character,
except she’s real.
Invisible Cyber Assassin Sam-R-I,
otherwise known as Samantha MacDuffie.

You better not cheat.
You better not lie.
You better not tweet.

I'm telling you why:
Sam-R-I is hunting
you down.

The virtual world of the 22nd century
is cluttered with everyone's digital graffiti.

Every March Fourth,
Sam-R-I chooses three people
whom she spies betraying
the untitled holiday spirit
by using their smartphone,
and she expunges their virtual presence:
passwords,
email accounts,
websites,
social media profiles,
avatars…
deleting everything you thought was you,
and yet you still remain.

She sees you when you’re texting.
and she knows when you’re online.
She knows if you’ve been blogging or not,
so be honest or she’ll hack your mind.

In a virtual landscape
filled with virtual identities,
the only thing that’s real
is erasure.

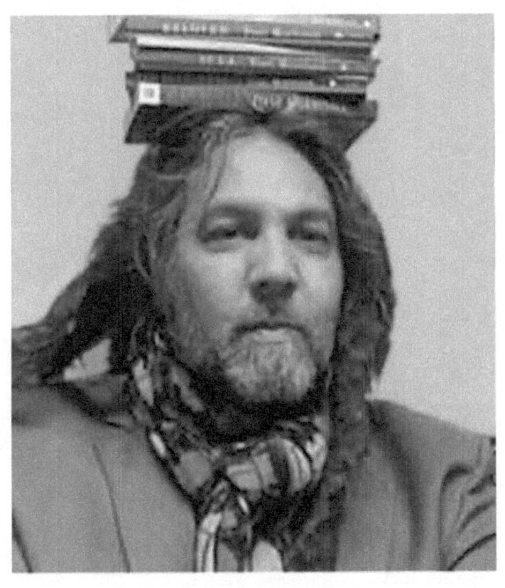

J. Martin Strangeweather tries his best to do what he thinks is right. What more do you want?

www.ingramcontent.com/pod-product-compliance
Lightning Source LLC
LaVergne TN
LVHW040351160726
843469LV00039B/673

* 9 7 8 0 5 7 8 3 9 8 4 8 8 *